T0137595

Developing Rhythmic Sensitivity
A Study Designed For All Musicians

WRITTEN BY

JACK BELL
COORDINATOR OF PERCUSSION STUDIES
GEORGIA STATE UNIVERSITY
RETIRED 2001

AND

HOWARD RYERSON DAVIS III
COMPOSER, ARTIST, AND VIDEO EDITOR

Order this book online at www.trafford.com
or email orders@trafford.com

Most Trafford titles are also available at major online book retailers.

Printed in the United States of America.

ISBN: 978-1-4269-6008-6 (sc)
ISBN: 978-1-4269-6009-3 (e)

Trafford rev. 02/17/2012

 www.trafford.com

North America & international
toll-free: 1 888 232 4444 (USA & Canada)
phone: 250 383 6864 ♦ fax: 812 355 4082

Biographical Information

 **Jack Bell** served as coordinator of percussion studies at Georgia State University from 1967 to 2001. Many of his more than 140 graduates now hold prominent symphonic, university, freelance, and business positions in the music industry throughout the United States. While at Georgia State, Mr. Bell created a new music course and textbook: Developing Rhythmic Sensitivity. As former principal percussionist with the Atlanta Symphony Orchestra for 32 years, Mr. Bell's performing credits include over 7,000 concerts, 43 world premiers, 65 recordings and 18 Grammy awards. He has been the recipient of many personal awards and recognitions throughout his career including: Outstanding People Of The 20th Century, 1998; International Who's Who of Intellectuals, 1998; Marquis Who's Who in America, 54th edition, 1999; and Lexington Who's Who Publications, 2000 edition. Mr. Bell's primary teachers were Harold Firestone and Cloyd Duff. He has been on the faculty of Gainesville State College in Oakwood, Georgia. Currently Mr. Bell is the Executive Director of the ProMusica Concert Series, Inc.

 **Howard Davis** has worked as a violinist, composer, stained glass artist, and inventor. He was trained as a composer and violinist at the North Carolina School of the Arts where he studied violin with Erick Friedman and composition with Robert Ward. Further studies were with Ulysses S. Kay and John Know. During the late 1970s and early 1980s he composed and performed music for concerts, television, theater, and film. For almost thirty years he designed and built stained glass windows for homes and churches. Recently he has work for Vubotics, Inc. as an inventor developing a new method for displaying text on a computer controlled electronic screen. He recently developed video editing abilities to create sport training videos that work on the subconscious level to improve athletic ability.

Acknowledgements

The contents of this book exist as a result of the dedicated and collective efforts offered by the following individuals:

Howard Ryerson Davis III - Composing rhythmic patterns and editing text

Kathy Banks - Typing and editing of text

April Bell - Contributing to and editing of text

Judith Rice - Editing Text

Sharon Salyer - Master Copy Editor

Dana Yeary - Editing Final Text

Paul Creston's book: <u>Principles of Rhythm</u>

Students at Georgia State University-"Related Concepts"

Concept Therapy Institute - Concept for "The Law of Rhythm"

Rick Kvistad - Inspiration for Counter Rhythm Worksheets

PREFACE

We live in an ocean of motion. Everything in our universe is moving in rhythm with everything else. Whether swinging in and out, moving forward and backward, or having a low and high tide, nothing is still. Every action has a reaction. When something advances, something must retreat. When one thing rises, another must sink. All of these are but individual expressions of one of the great natural laws of our universe: **The Law of Rhythm!**

This law can be observed in part on the physical level by the change of seasons, night and day, or rain and sunshine. It may be observed in the mental-emotional realms through the rhythmic swings of negative and positive expressions of thought. In music, **The Law of Rhythm** is the nucleus of the creative process.

Composers use the musical elements to create dissonance and consonance, tension and release, symmetry and imbalance. Conductors and performers re-create or interpret the composer's intentions. Interpretation is a subjective process, but at its foundation must be an objective or literal understanding of the noted musical symbols. Even though tempo and nuance may vary with each performance, pitches and rhythm remain constant. And rhythm is still the cornerstone!

Through rhythm, body movements become dance, words become poetry and **sounds become music. Rhythm in music** is an audible measure of time, but an intangible object in space. It is dependent upon the proper functioning and interpretation of each person's "internal clock." Often it is a difficult task to objectively measure an intangible distance into 2, 3, 4, 5 or more properly spaced parts. <u>Therefore, the purpose of this book is to help musicians interpret all rhythms more accurately through a precise understanding of noted, objective rhythm.</u>

Jack Bell

Table of Contents

     A. Introduction to Rhythm

     B. Understanding the Elements of Rhythm

     C. Learning Rhythms

     D. Related Concepts

     Rhythm Is...

     Energy Is...

     Concentration Is...

     Confidence Is...

     Coordination Is...

     Creativity Is...

     Jazz Style

GLOSSARY OF TERMS

Accent-emphasizes a pulse or rhythmic pattern and helps it to become more prominent.

Changing rhythmic structure-occurs when the measures of a composition are organized into pulse groups of unequal duration and the measures do not all contain the same number of pulses.

Complex rhythmic pattern-changing rhythmic pattern.

Fraction meter signatures-add to or reduce the traditional number of pulses in a meter signature.

Free rhythmic structure-exists when the measures of a composition contain rhythmic patterns that are allowed to fluctuate freely in pace.

Imaging rhythms-ability to mentally conceive or perceive rhythmic patterns.

Irregular rhythmic pattern-results when a noted rhythmic pattern is not a naturally occurring division or subdivision of the pulse.

Measured rhythmic structure-formed when all the measures of a composition contain the same number of pulses and the distance between implied primary and secondary stressed pulses is **not the same.**

Meter-the grouping of pulses in one or more measures of time.

Meter signatures-visual symbols through which musical sounds in time are organized and noted.

Metric modulation-compositional technique for gradually changing from one meter to another.

Metrical rhythmic structure-formed when all the measures of a composition contain the same number of pulses and the distance between implied primary and secondary stressed pulses is the **same.**

Objective rhythms-rhythms that are noted.

Objective time-clock-time; founded on the objective universe.

Pace - speed at which the pulses of a measure of time occur.

Primary pulse/primary dynamic stress - natural accentuation of the first pulse in a measure of time.

Pulses - equally spaced distances in measured time.

Regular rhythmic pattern - rhythmic pattern in which there is a normal division or subdivision of the pulse.

Rhythmic patterns - noted, played rhythms in measured time.

Rhythm - organization of durations in time comprised of meter, pace, and accent.

Simple rhythmic pattern - repeated rhythmic pattern.

Sound and time - basic materials necessary to produce rhythm in music.

Subjective rhythms - rhythms conceived by mind of composer and interpreted by minds of conductor, performer, or teacher.

Subjective time - time as it exists within the mind.

Units - smallest practical divisions and subdivisions of the rhythmic patterns in measured time.

Developing Rhythmic Sensitivity

A study designed for all musicians

A. **Introduction to Rhythm**
B. **Understanding the Elements of Rhythm**
C. **Learning Rhythms**
D. **Related Concepts**

A. Introduction to Rhythm

What are the two basic materials necessary to produce rhythm in music?

Why?

Rhythm in music is everything that pertains to the length of time or duration of the musical sound. Therefore, **sound** and **time** are the two basic materials necessary to produce rhythm in music.

Sound: We are continuously surrounded by sounds. The slightest vibrations of matter disturb the air and produce sound. Some sounds are not audible because their high or low frequencies are past our levels of awareness. Other sounds, such as the annoying buzz made by the wings of a nearby fly or mosquito can be heard, but the pace of their flapping wings is much too fast to be perceived as a rhythm. Only by slowing down the pace in time of those flapping wings could we begin to hear the rhythms being produced.

Time: Human beings have come to experience time in **two ways**. Time is most often thought of as **clock time.** Train, plane, navigation schedules, and telecommunication all depend on accurate time standards. These standards are based upon the revolution of the earth around the sun and by the earth's rotation upon its axis. Because this concept of time is founded upon the objective universe, it is called **objective time.** From old grandfather clocks, to modern day wrist watches, **the purpose of a time keeping device is to objectively divide the 24 hour period of** day and night into hours, minutes, seconds, and parts of a second.

We know, however, from our personal experiences--musical and otherwise, that time does not always feel to be passing evenly under all circumstances. When we are in the midst of an exciting activity, time seems to move very quickly, but when we are waiting in a traffic-jam, time seems to move very slowly. This concept is based upon time existing only within the mind and is called **subjective time.**

How do these two concepts of time relate to rhythm?

1. Rhythm in objective time:

2. Rhythm in subjective time:

In music, **rhythm is the organization of durations in time.** It exists both objectively and subjectively. **Objective rhythms** are noted. **Subjective rhythms** are noted rhythms **interpreted by the mind** of the musician. The proportions of objective rhythms are exact and occur in relation to objective time.
Because subjective rhythms must be interpreted by the mind of the musician, they are inaccurate and occur in relation to subjective time. Therefore, in the creation and performance of rhythmic patterns, the following cycle exists:

1. Rhythms are subjectively conceived in the mind of a composer...
2. Those rhythms become...
3. Objective through the resulting noted rhythmic patterns...
4. The noted rhythmic patterns become...
5. Subjectively interpreted by the mind of the conductor, performer, or teacher.

The major purpose of this book is to help musicians interpret all rhythms more accurately through a precise understanding of noted objective rhythm.

B. Understanding the Elements of Rhythm

Rhythm in music is the organization of durations in time. It is comprised of three elements: **meter, pace,** and **accent.** (See summary charts at the end of this section.)

METER

Meter is the grouping of pulses in one or more measures of time. For our purposes, meter will be divided into two concepts: **meter signatures,** often called time signatures, and **four types of larger rhythmic structures.**

Meter signatures are visual symbols through which musical sounds in time can be organized and noted. These symbols determine how the sounds are organized through their association with pulses, rhythmic patterns, and units. **Pulses** are the equally spaced distances in measured time. **Rhythmic patterns** are the noted, played rhythms in measured time. **Units** are the smallest practical divisions and subdivisions of the rhythmic patterns in measured time. Consider the following examples utilizing these three components of meter as defined above:

Example A:

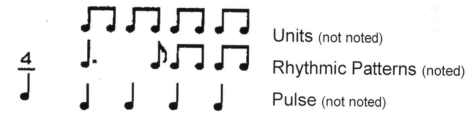

Units (not noted)

Rhythmic Patterns (noted)

Pulse (not noted)

Example B:

Units (not noted)

Rhythmic Patterns (noted)

Pulse (not noted)

Rhythmic patterns are classified **as regular or irregular,** and as **simple** or **complex.** A repeated rhythmic pattern is **simple (CI),** a changing rhythmic pattern is **complex (C2).**

Example C:

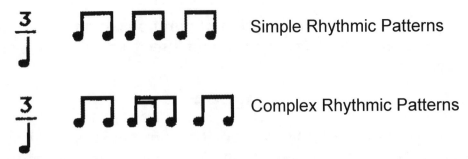

Simple Rhythmic Patterns

Complex Rhythmic Patterns

A rhythmic pattern in which there is a normal division or subdivision of the pulse is classified **as a regular rhythmic pattern (D1).** When the noted rhythm is not a naturally occurring division or subdivision of the pulse, it is classified as an **irregular rhythmic pattern (D2).**

Note: (DI) A normal division of a simple meter is two equal parts. A normal subdivision of a simple meter is four, eight etc. parts. A normal division of a compound meter is three equal parts. A normal subdivision of a compound meter is six, twelve, etc. equal parts.

Example D:

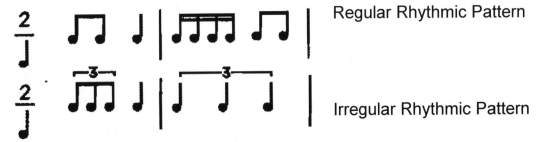

Regular Rhythmic Pattern

Irregular Rhythmic Pattern

The following example shows the four classifications of rhythmic patterns:

Example E:

Four types of larger rhythmic structures comprise the second part of meter. They are as follows: **Metrical structure, measured structure, changing structure,** and **free structure.**

A **metrical rhythmic structure** is formed when all the measures of a composition contain the same number of pulses and the distance between implied primary and secondary stressed pulses is the **same.** For example, in a 4/4 meter the four equally spaced pulses occur with an implied primary and secondary stress on the first and third pulse of every measure.

A **measured rhythmic structure** is formed when all the measures of a composition contain the same number of pulses and the distance between implied primary and secondary stressed pulses is **not the same.** This principle is easily identified in meters like 5/4 and 7/4. In a 5/4 meter, for example, the five equally spaced pulses occur with an implied primary stress on the first pulse of every measure and a secondary implied stress on the third (2+3) **or** the fourth (3+2) pulse of every measure.

Rhythmic patterns strongly influence perception of metrical and measured rhythmic structures. For example, when an eighth note rhythmic pattern of 3+3+2 occurs in a 4/4 meter, **subjectively,** the distance between implied primary and secondary stressed pulses is **perceived to** be **unequal-a measured rhythmic structure (♩.♩.♩).** **Objectively,** however, the distance between implied primary and secondary stressed pulses is **still the same - a metrical rhythmic structure.** Interestingly, this effective grouping of eighth notes has been a favorite from medieval times to the present and is the basic rhythm of the Cuban rumba.

A **changing rhythmic structure** occurs when the measures of a composition are organized into pulse groups of unequal duration and the measures do not **all** contain the same number of pulses. A changing rhythmic structure would **be more** commonly known as a composition of changing meter or changing time signatures.

A **free rhythmic structure** exists when the measures of a composition (if measures exist at all) contain rhythmic patterns that are allowed to fluctuate freely in pace. Thus, the free rhythmic structure becomes less strictly organized with regard to the steady pulse-rhythmic pattern relationships found in the other three rhythmic structures. Musical terms appropriately associated with a free rhythmic structure are accelerando, rallentando, or the term rubato. A rubato creates the occurrence of an accelerando or rallentando without greatly altering the pace rate of the pulse.

Free rhythmic structures also include a number of rhythmic concepts well outside the necessary parameters of this book. However, there are two other free rhythmic structure devices we will consider briefly: metric modulation and fraction meter signatures. Metric modulation (Example F) is a compositional technique for gradually changing from one meter to another.

Example F:

♩ = 40–50 MM

Fraction meter signatures (Example G) add to or reduce the traditional number of pulses in a measure of time. This meter signature is a visual device for a 9/8 meter with the majority of the measure being grouped traditionally.

Example G:

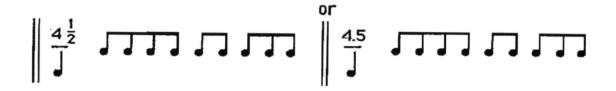

Summary: **Rhythmic patterns must be practical in notation.** Experimenting with the mass of mathematical possibilities in notation is often not rhythmically or musically effective. Regardless of how fascinating a rhythm appears to be on paper, **if it is not practical to the eye and mind of the performer, it is a waste of valuable writing and performing time!**

PACE

Pace, in music, is the speed at which the pulses of a measure of time occur. Often, pace seems to be influenced by meter signatures or by rhythmic patterns (Example H). For example, when playing rhythmic patterns in a meter signature that is the symbol for a longer measure of time, such as 4/4 (H1) and 12/8 (H3) the pulses may appear to occur at a slower rate of pace than when playing the same rhythmic patterns in a meter signature that is the symbol for a shorter measure of time, such as 2/4 (H2) and 6/8 (H4). The actual occurrence rate of the pulses is the same for 4/4 and 2/4 or for 12/8 and 6/8, but since the **primary pulses or primary dynamic stresses** (naturally accented or first to occur in a measure of time) are more widely spaced in the longer measures of time, a subtle illusion of slower pulse occurrence is created.

Example H:

Likewise, longer rhythmic patterns, such as half and quarter notes (Example I: 1) often give the feeling of a slower rate of pulse occurrence. While in contrast, a shorter rhythmic pattern like sixteenth notes (Example I: 2) over the same pulse, gives the feeling of a faster rate of pulse occurrence.

Example I:

* — Primary pulse .

Admittedly, the illusion of differences in the speed of pulse occurrence is subtle, but it does exist.

ACCENT

Accent, the third element of rhythm, emphasizes a pulse or rhythmic pattern and helps it to become more prominent. Without accents, meter often becomes a monotonous series of pulses, pace can lose its sense of forward motion, and rhythmic patterns can become difficult to interpret or to articulate.

Consider some of the different effects **of the primary pulses or primary dynamic stresses** on the following rhythmic pattern (Example J). This pattern will not sound the same when the duration of time between **primary dynamic stresses** is altered (J1 and J2). A different sound will result when pick-up notes displace the **primary dynamic stresses** to a new position within the rhythmic pattern (J3 and J4). In a series of changing meter signatures, (J5) the irregularity of the **primary dynamic stresses** varies the sound of the rhythmic pattern yet again.

In order to experience the different sounds of Example J: 1 - 5 count out loud and clap each example.

*- indicates primary pulse or dynamic stress point

Accents are often thought of in terms of **dynamic stress** or **tone intensity** alone.

These are the more obvious and elementary types of accents, but often there are other, more subtle ways to make all or part of the pitches occurring on various rhythmic patterns more prominent.

A classification of accent types, beginning with the most easily identified, and moving toward the various more subtle types follows. There are, at the very least, nine types of accent.

1. **The dynamic accent** emphasizes a pulse or rhythmic pattern through an intensity of tone. Noted *as* >, ^, or sfz, this accent is the most elementary and most easily understood accent type. It is dependent upon being produced by the performer more than being produced by the nature of the musical structure itself.

2. **The agogic accent** is an accent of duration. It is produced by playing a particular tone longer than the tones preceding or following it. At least two methods help to make one tone seem longer than its surrounding tones: placing a short note before the note to be emphasized and repeating the emphasized tone.

3. **The metric accent** is produced by a rhythmic pattern that occurs at the same rate of pace as the pulses, thus it helps to emphasize the primary and secondary pulse in each measure of time (i.e. a rhythmic pattern of three quarter notes in a 3/4 meter signature).

4. **The harmonic accent** is an accent produced by a dissonance that occurs on the pulse intended to be stressed.

5. **The weight accent** is created as a result of more sound added to the musical texture in order to produce greater volume.

6. **The pitch accent** is created at the point of the highest or lowest pitch, in a series of tones. Generally, a greater distance between the highest and lowest tones produces a more effective pitch accent.

7. **The pattern accent** occurs at the point where a series of notes repeat themselves in an exact, or in a similar motion.

8. **The embellished accent** is created by an embellishment of the melodic line. An apoggiatura, acciaccatura, mordent or trills are all examples of embellished accents.

9. **The tone-color accent** is expressed when a notable color change can be heard through the surrounding sounds. An example of a tone-color accent would be a triangle stroke that occurs during a string passage.

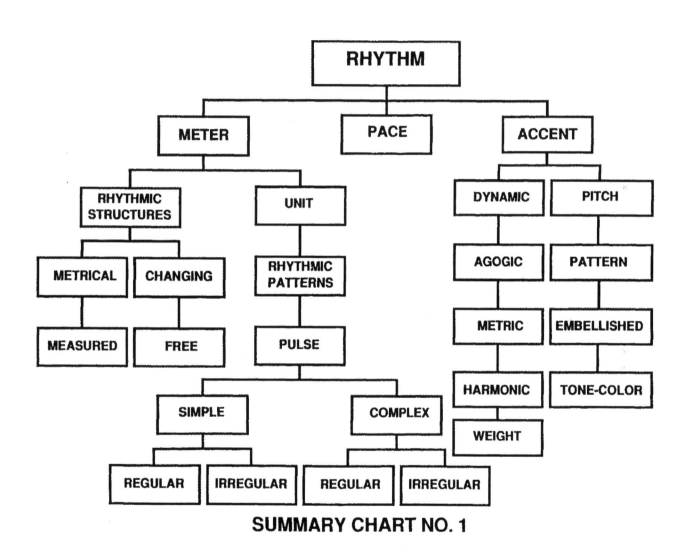

SUMMARY CHART NO. 1

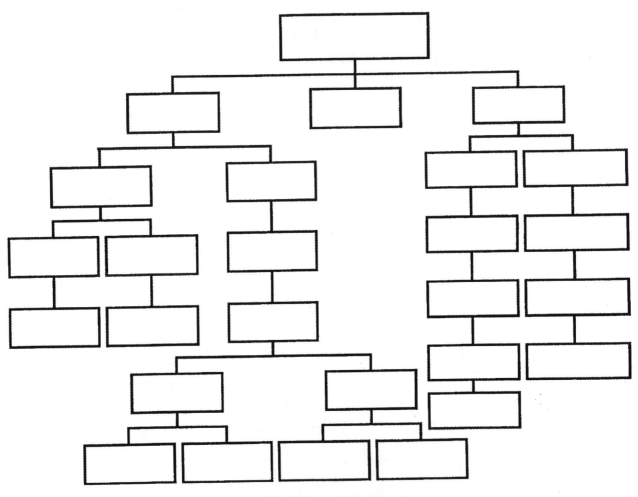

SUMMARY CHART NO. 2

C. Learning Rhythms

As musicians we have all gone through various learning processes when we attempt to master a new technique or to improve a tone. A similar process is evident in the mastery of rhythms as well. The beginning musician may be introduced to rhythms through word association or simply by imitating the rhythmic sounds produced by other musicians. At best, some "guesstimation" on the part of the student is involved. I call this the **illogical process of estimation.** It is not wrong, but it is simply not a complete process as it is dependent upon association and imitation. Learning rhythmic patterns through the illogical process of estimation is reminiscent of a piece of **Swiss cheese: filled with a lot of big holes!** As students becomes more technically competent, they shift to the **mathematical process** in order to improve rhythmic accuracy. At this stage of development, the rhythms produced will be technically calculated, very unemotional, and at times tense and insensitive to the needs of the music. Learning to count mathematically is a necessary second step to becoming a rhythmically competent performer. At an advanced level, the student approaches rhythm through a **logical process of estimation.** All techniques are grounded in solid mathematical concepts, but are performed in a much more relaxed, free and natural manner. The performance sound has more of an improvised quality and the student's conceptual understanding of rhythm is now **homogenized!** Even for the most accomplished musician, a particular rhythm may seem so unfamiliar that it ends up being performed at the level of illogical estimation. In fact, if truthful, most musicians find that their rhythmic abilities often span all three levels of rhythmic competency, depending upon the difficulty of a given rhythm.

Improving potential rhythmic abilities enough to perform all rhythms equally well involves many insights. Here are five:

1. **Attention to details**
2. **Understanding musical math**
3. **Imaging rhythms**
4. **Verbalizing the images**
5. **Maintaining a steady pace**

After reading the brief orientation statement and examples of each of these five insights, expand your own rhythmic abilities by actively applying them to various pieces of music.

ATTENTION TO DETAILS

1. Attention to details is almost self-explanatory, but it is seldom followed, especially by younger students. **Assume nothing when reading through a page of rhythms!** In fact, consider every note of every measure to be wrong and prove them to be right, rather than casually accepting that they are probably right from the beginning of the piece. Mentally confirm, and physically perform every dynamic change, especially those that are more subtle such as **pp** to **p** or **f** to **ff**. Read the following phrase out loud:

    The cat and
    and the dog.

    Pay attention to details!

    (Incorrect and correct versions of "attention to detail" sheets

    follow Example K.)

UNDERSTANDING MUSICAL MATH

2. Understanding musical math is always a necessary step toward becoming a rhythmically competent performer. Properly applying the concepts of musical math to rhythmic performance is often difficult. Because rhythm is an audible measure of time, but an intangible object in space, it is dependent upon the proper functioning and interpretation of each person's "internal clock." Each person is expected to measure objectively an intangible distance in space and time and to divide that distance into 2, 3, 4, 5 or more properly spaced parts. Therefore, each performer must establish a personal, logical, and valid system for counting rhythmic patterns, regardless of the rhythmic pattern's intricacy.

Remember:

A. All systems used to count rhythmic patterns, especially those used to count the smaller divisions of a pulse, contain inherent counting difficulties.

B. All systems used to count rhythmic patterns need to be adjusted to fit the abilities of each performer.

C. Any rhythmic pattern may require using parts of a number of different counting systems. Various counting systems are shown in Example K.

Example K:

MY (JB)
PREFERENCE:

MY (HRD)
PREFERENCE:

READER'S
PREFERENCE:

• BE CAREFUL OF PULSATIONS OR FALSE ACCENTS
* TWO SYLLABLE WORD-TRY "SEVN"

Attention to Details-Incorrect Version

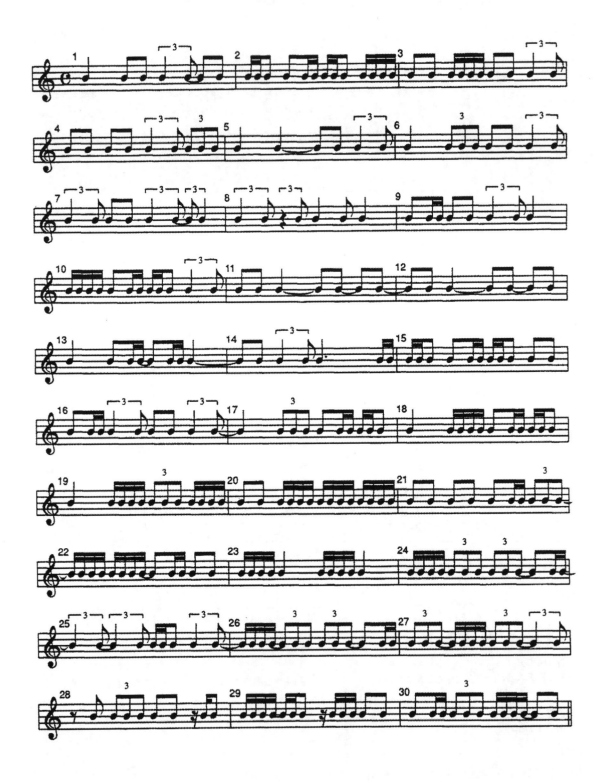

Attention to Details-Correct Version

A good "method" for improving abilities in musical math is using phone numbers! Select any phone number and proceed as follows...

Example L:

1. Take each number and assign rhythmic relationships as shown in Example L.

2. Write out the related rhythmic pattern for each digit of the given phone number.

3. Assign a specific counting system to each of the noted rhythmic patterns.

4. Count these rhythmic patterns aloud at a pace of a quarter note at 40 mm. Reduce the inflection in your voice. Speak in a distinct chant style and articulate each note individually.

5. Clap or tap the rhythmic pattern as you count aloud.

6. Repeat this process until you literally hear a voice-type playback of the entire rhythmic pattern in your mind.

7. Apply these same steps to other phone numbers

Example M shows steps 1-3 of this process. Try chanting and clapping this phone number.

Example M: 732-1546 ♩ = 40 mm (including various counting options)

	BARBAQUE POTATOCHIP	TRIPOLET	MILKSHAKE	NOTE	HIPPOPOTAMUS	MISSISSIPPI	ONOMATOPOEIA
	1 2 3 4 5 6 7 *	1 2 3	1 2	1	1 2 3 4 5	1 2 3 4	1 2 3 4 5 6
	•1 2 3 4 1 2 3				•1 2 1 2 3		
	•1 2 3 1 2 3 4				•1 2 3 1 2		
	1 2 3 4 5 6 7 *	2 2 3	3 2	4	5 2 3 4 5	6 2 3 4	7 2 3 4 5 6

MY (JB)
PREFERENCE: 1 2 3 4 5 6 7 * TATATATATATATA / 2 0 LET TATATA / 3 AN TATA / 4 TA / 5 2 3 4 5 TATATATATA / 6 DEANDA TATATATA / 7 0LETANOLET TATATATATATA TATAKATATAKA

MY (HRD)
PREFERENCE: 1 TEEDEEDEE&TADA | 2 & DA | 3 & | 4 | 5 DEE&TADA / 5 TEEDEE&DA | 6 DE & DA | 7 DE & DA & DA / 7 TE DE & TA DA

READER'S PREFERENCE:

• BE CAREFUL OF PULSATIONS OR FALSE ACCENTS   * TWO SYLABLE WORD—TRY "SEVN"

Meter Signatures And Note Value Relationships

Meter Signatures

Developing abilities in musical math also requires an understanding of both **meter signatures and of note value relationships. Meter signatures are visual symbols through which musical sounds in time are organized and noted.** The numerator of a meter signature shows the total number of pulses occurring in one measure of time. (2/duple, 3/triple, 4/quadruple, 5/quintuple, etc.) The denominator of a meter signature shows the kind of note that receives one of those pulses in a measure of time. The terms **simple, compound and complex** refer to the manner in which the rate of pulse occurrence is traditionally divided and conducted.

With the number 15 as a logical parameter, the numerator of **simple meter signatures** will be 1, 2, 3, 4, or 8 (1/1, 2/2, 3/4, 4/16), 8/8). In **simple meter signatures** (2/4, 3/4, 4/4, etc.) at a slow pace, the conducted pulses are often divided into two equally spaced notes with each note conducted separately. In these same **simple meter signatures** at a **moderate pace,** the pulses are conducted. At a **fast pace** either the pulses will be conducted or 1 conducting beat will occur for every evenly spaced group of 2 or 3 pulses.

Again, using the number 15 as the outer boundary, the numerators **of compound meter signatures** will be 6, 9, 12, or 15 (6/4, 9/16, 12/8, 15/32). In **compound**

meter signatures at a **slow pace,** the pulses are conducted. At both a **moderate** and **fast pace,** the pulses of **compound meter signatures** are conducted in equally spaced groups of three (3).

Finally, using the same number 15, the numerators of **complex meter signatures will** be 5, 7, 10, 11, 13, and 14 (5/8, 7/4, 10/32, 11/8, 13/4, 14/16). In **complex meter signatures** at a **slow pace,** the conducted pulses are either divided into two equally spaced notes, with each note conducted separately or the pulses are conducted, such as in a slow 5/8 or 7/16 measure of time. In **moderately paced complex meters,** either the pulses will be conducted or one conducting beat will occur for every evenly spaced group of two or three pulses. Finally, in **complex meter signatures at a fast pace,** the pulses will usually be conducted in evenly spaced groups of two and three pulses each.

Note Value Relationships

Note value relationships are the final area of musical math to be considered. Understanding these relationships is a necessary requirement for performing many of the easier and the more complicated rhythmic patterns accurately. The mathematical basis for all rhythm is found in the following example:

Example N:

Any rhythm or meter signature, no matter how complicated, can usually be seen as a multiple, division, or composite (as found in counter or polyrhythmic figures) of Example N. For example, the meter signature 5/8 can be broken down into traditional pulse groupings of 2 + 3, 3 + 2, 2 + 2 + 1, etc. 7/8 can exist in any one of the following common patterns: 3 + 4, 4 + 3, 2 + 3 + 2, 2 + 2 + 3 etc. Two of an unlimited number of example questions regarding note value relationships follow:

A.   If a dotted quarter note equals a metronome marking of 80, what is the pace of a quarter note? (120 pulses per minute) Why? (Both examples equal 240 eighth notes per minute. The dotted quarter note equals 80 groups of 3 eighth notes each or 240 eighth notes per minute. The quarter note equals 120 groups of 2 eighth notes each or 240 eighth notes per minute.)

B.   If a dotted eighth note equals a metronome marking of 96, what is the metronome marking of a dotted quarter note? (48 pulses per minute) Why? (A dotted eighth note equals 3 sixteenth notes or 288 sixteenth notes each minute. A dotted quarter note equals 6 sixteenth notes each time it occurs. Therefore 288 divided by 6 equals 48 occurrences of the dotted quarter note per minute or a metronome marking of 48.)

IMAGING RHYTHMS

Imaging rhythms is the ability to mentally conceive or perceive rhythmic patterns. Once a rhythmic pattern has been imaged correctly in the mind of the composer or performer, it can then be written or performed accurately. The skill of imaging rhythmic patterns successfully is dependent upon improving the ability of the "mind's ear" to convert noted images into sounds. The more one's mind can associate sounds with their related noted images, the easier the imaging process becomes. In the study of music theory, "rhythmic dictation" is a common title for the process of imaging rhythmic patterns. Thus, "taking rhythmic dictation" is the learned ability to translate the mental image of a rhythmic pattern into its related noted symbol. The process of imaging rhythmic patterns or taking dictation often begins with "helpful hints" such as being given a meter signature, the number of measures, the existence of pick-up notes, or by simply writing note heads without durations etc. When rhythmic sensitivity is sufficient, actual rhythmic symbols are added such as different types of note heads, stems, bars, dots and ties, etc. Gradually, the number and length of the measures to be imaged can be increased and the "helpful hints" decreased. Learning to image rhythms is similar to an earlier successful process of learning to read words. First grade students are not assigned an epic length novel to read on the first day of school. Instead, they are taught individual letters, then words and finally phrases, sentences and entire paragraphs. In the same manner, the student attempting to develop an ability to image rhythms should not expect to image whole phrases at the beginning. Instead, a student should "take dictation" regularly, so that through guided practice over a period of time, the abilities necessary to the process of imaging will fully develop.

VERBALIZING THE IMAGES

Verbalizing the images means that the composer or performer is to verbally describe conceived or perceived rhythmic patterns. The description must be brief and accurate. It may range from effective analogies to precise mathematical explanations. The language used must paint a clear mental picture for the listener. As a result, all aspects of the various rhythmic patterns will be thoroughly understood as they are discussed. Developing an ability to verbalize rhythmic patterns is enhanced by regularly listening to, imitating, and describing all kinds of rhythmic sounds, both musical and non-musical.

Non-musical rhythmic patterns are found in the sounds of nature, rickety machinery, a watch, a pile driver, poetry or spoken words and word phrases, etc. For example, the syllables of the word Takita (Tah-kee-tah) may be grouped in ways that create rhythmic patterns that are verbalized as being sharp, jagged, rough, tense or angry sounding (ie., various combinations of eighth notes, dotted eighth notes, and sixteenth notes in a 2/4 meter, at a fast pace). In contrast, the syllables of the word Malooma (Mah-loo-mah) seem to be softer and more relaxed. They might be described verbally by the words: round, soft, kind, gentle, or smooth and they might be represented by rhythmic patterns that are various combinations of eighth and quarter notes in a 6/8 meter, at a moderate pace.

In addition to the non-musical rhythmic patterns, many other more traditional rhythms are available for listening to, imitating, and verbally describing music. Examples include music performed at a concert, on the radio and television or by the singing, clapping, and tapping of various rhythmic patterns, etc.

It is often difficult, but necessary to avoid vagueness, generalizations, and assumptions when verbalizing the mathematical relationships that are contained in various rhythmic patterns. For example, a common definition given for a symbol related to a rhythmic pattern is the definition of a dot (.). It is usually stated as follows: A dot increases the value of a note or rest by one-half of its original value. This established definition, although brief, is hard to image clearly without out more detailed explanation. What is the actual value of a note or rest? How do you increase that value by one-half? Let's try to verbalize the image more clearly (Example 0). First, the value of a note or rest is the length of its sound or its duration. Actual length of sound is determined by dividing or subdividing the note into 2, 3, 4, or smaller equally spaced notes that have the same total duration as the original note. To determine the original note's value or duration, divide the note into two equally spaced notes of the next smallest division. To increase the value of the note or rest by one-half of its original value, add one of those two equally spaced notes from the next smallest division onto the original note's value or its length of sound; thus, the dotted note becomes one-third longer in duration than the same note without a dot.

Example O:

One example of a more difficult rhythmic pattern to image and verbalize is as follows:

Example P:

Three equally spaced quarter notes are occurring in the same duration of time as two equally spaced quarter notes (Example Q). The intrinsic value of the three quarter notes cannot be changed. They are always equal in duration to six eighth notes (Q1). If the quarter notes are grouped under a triplet symbol, then the eighth notes they are equal to will also be grouped under triplet symbols (Q2). The natural, normal grouping of six eighth notes under two triplet symbols in a simple meter signature is two groups of three eighth notes each (Q2). This rhythmic pattern changes the natural grouping of the six eighth notes from 2 groups of 3 eighth notes each to 3 groups of 2 eighth notes each (Q3). Primarily, a simple shifting of accent has occurred (Q4). This is one of the important principles involved in playing many counter or polyrhythms.

Example Q:

MAINTAINING A STEADY PACE

The ability to maintain a steady pace is necessary in order to perform rhythmic patterns successfully. Pace, the speed at which the pulses of a measure of time occur is first an objective, unchanging, and evenly divided measurement of time. Internalizing and consciously maintaining a steady pace when performing is the basis upon which musical phrasings and rhythmical interpretations are successfully built. But pace, as it relates to musical performance, must also be a subjective experience that often allows the pulse to fluctuate freely within the musical phrase, as in an accelerando, rallentando and rubato. Arbitrarily maintaining only a steady pace whenever performing will often result in a technically calculated, unemotional and often tense performance that is insensitive to the needs of the music (the mathematical process). Finding the proper balance between regularity and freedom of pace requires the best efforts of an experienced *and* sensitive performer. However, the ability to maintain a steady pace is the foundation for a more musically sensitive performance, therefore, the performer must first establish a valid concept of steady pace. To understand the meaning of steady pace, use a metronome. It is the best source for an unemotional, unchanging, external pulse. It is relentlessly steady and when used consciously and consistently, it will help to develop accurate and steady rhythmic performance. Here are some simple, effective metronome exercises:

1. Spend time simply listening to a metronome clicking at various speeds (3 or more minutes at a time).
2. Turn the metronome off and mentally continue to hear those clicks occurring with perfectly equal spacing.
3. Listen to the metronome and imagine accents that group the pulses in various ways; for example, in groups of 4 pulses with an imagined accent on 1, or on 1 and 3, or on 2 and 4 etc. Create artificial accents that group the pulses in groups of 5, with an imagined accent on 1 and 3 or on 1 and 4 etc.
4. Count along with a metronome's clicks out loud in a chant-like style, i.e. accenting and individualizing each click. Then with the metronome set at a slower pace, (40-60 mm) clap with the clicks and try to block out the sound of at least 5 clicks in a row. Also, try to block out the sound of various clicks 1 through 5.
5. Play a series of rhythmic patterns with the metronome clicking the primary pulses in a traditional manner.
6. Play those same rhythmic patterns with the clicking of the metronome occurring on the "off or after beat" rather than "on the beat."

7. Then play those same rhythmic patterns with the clicking of the metronome occurring on the fourth or on the second sixteenth of each pulse.
8. Record the entire practice procedure and listen to the playback carefully and critically. **Good Luck!**

D. Related Concepts

Finally, rhythm is better understood through an intense study of some of its many related concepts: **energy, concentration, confidence, coordination** and **creativity.** Each concept will occur in more detail later in this book.

Section I

RHYTHM IS...

Rhythm in music is the organization of durations in time. It is comprised of three elements: **meter, pace,** and **accent.** J.B.

Rhythm is a fundamental facet of our universe. From the sub microscopic atom to the galaxies of the macro universe, all are related to each other through time in a universal rhythm. Through the rhythms of music we create our own universes of sound. We order pitch to create our scales and harmonies (the rhythm of pitch); we order attacks and sustains to create our rhythms. H.R.D.

Student Definitions:

...Webster defines rhythm as being the recurrence or repetition of stress, beat, sound, accent, motion, etc. actually occurring in a regular or harmonious pattern or manner...present in the rising and setting of the sun, in the act of breathing, in the sequence of waking and sleeping...in the arrangement of windows in a building, in the pattern of pickets in a fence...Several elements each of the above illustrations have in common: 1) a background which may consist of either time or space, 2) an event or detail that occurs repeatedly, 3) a decisive factor that separates one event or detail from the next, 4) some form or relationship between each repetition. Rhythm results from the consistent recurrence of an event or detail that breaks up the formless background of time or space into convenient units. Rhythm is a principle that enables us to recognize or bring order into our perception of time and space...

...Melody and harmony unfold together. They have to move forward together in rhythm. Rhythm is the orderly movement of music in time. Rhythm springs from the need for order that is in every one of us...

...If space is a necessary concept of physical life, then time is the necessary counterpart for our mental lives. Everything we do is done in time. Without it, life would vanish, and so would music. But time has not vanished, and in its ever elusive omnipresence, we measure out the duration of our lives with it. For the sake of semantics, it is important to remember that the word time is merely a means of describing something which our senses indicate to us as existing. It is indicated to us in the most profound ways of which the most accessible is day and night. In this one never-ending cycle, one sees the characteristics which constitute a definition of time. These characteristics include patterns (cycles), regularity, duration, recurrence, succession, and above all motion. Rhythm pulls these elements into more specific terms. Rhythm takes the concept of time and breaks it down into equal lengths of duration by which we can measure events. In music that event is sound. Rhythm measures in regular (equal) pulses, the duration of successive sounds. Because of time's characteristic of motion, and consequently rhythm's characteristic of motion, music would be nothing without it. As an illustration of this motion, consider a live performance. As each note is played and released it moves from the state of being, to a state of being a memory. As we listen, we can anticipate the sounds to be heard in the future. Now we can see where the time element is so important in a mental aspect. Rhythm (which is measured time) is the main tool by which we organize music, thus making our music intelligible, and consequently meaningful...

...The presumption that a precise definition can be stated implies that we can solidify an intangible entity whose components are tangible elements. Rhythm occurs on so many different levels--whether it is sounds, body movements, or the changing of seasons, that generalizations have to be very vague in order not to exclude any level of functioning. It provides the standard to judge how well a performance flowed and how rhythmically and interpretively secure the performer felt. In an ensemble situation, the above is also true, but rhythm becomes the unifying force between players--it enables the individuals to become one by providing the heartbeat to the en masse circulatory system. Rhythm seems to be a gestalt principle in that the whole cannot be defined by the sum of its parts. It is not just units, pulses, and patterns that constitute rhythms, although they are the essentials of developing a good sense of rhythm. Rhythms have to be intellectualized enough to be mathematically accurate, yet must become natural and comfortable enough to make a performer aware of the most delicate and subtle of imbalances...

...Rhythm is probably the single most important factor of our existence because how *well we* perform a given task is a direct consequence of the quality of rhythm we use in performing that task. For example, in order to make a double play on the baseball diamond, the second baseman must possess the knowledge and the capability of moving his body and feet from one position to another in one smooth, rhythmic motion in order to tag second base and throw the runner out at first. This is a very complex example of rhythm because there are several sounds involved within the movement--the rustle of the feet moving on the field, the pop of the ball into the glove, and the swinging of arms when throwing the ball. All of these rhythms together combine to form one rhythm --that of a double play. And what a pleasant sound it does make. Rhythm also affects the quality of performance in music. Music is sound created through time. Therefore, the effect rhythm has on music is the duration of each sound...

Preparatory Rhythmic Exercises

1. In the following exercises, the denominator represents the pulse.
2. The numerator represents an equal division of the pulse.
3. Using a specific counting system, (see example K) count aloud and clap or tap the numerator.
4. Practice daily with and without a metronome.

Sequential division of pulse:

$$\frac{2}{1}\ \frac{1}{1}\ \frac{2}{1}\ \frac{2}{1}\ \frac{3}{1}\ \frac{4}{1}\ \frac{2}{1}\ \frac{1}{1}\ \frac{2}{1}\ \frac{3}{1}\ \frac{2}{1}\ \frac{4}{1}\ \frac{1}{1}\ \frac{2}{1}\ \frac{3}{1}\ \frac{2}{1}\ \frac{1}{1}\ \frac{2}{1}\ \frac{3}{1}\ \frac{2}{1}\ \frac{1}{1}\ \frac{2}{1}\ \frac{4}{1}\ \frac{2}{1}$$

$$\frac{3}{1}\ \frac{2}{1}\ \frac{3}{1}\ \frac{3}{1}\ \frac{3}{1}\ \frac{4}{1}\ \frac{3}{1}\ \frac{2}{1}\ \frac{3}{1}\ \frac{1}{1}\ \frac{3}{1}\ \frac{3}{1}\ \frac{4}{1}\ \frac{3}{1}\ \frac{1}{1}\ \frac{3}{1}\ \frac{3}{1}\ \frac{2}{1}\ \frac{3}{1}\ \frac{3}{1}\ \frac{4}{1}\ \frac{3}{1}\ \frac{2}{1}\ \frac{3}{1}$$

$$\frac{4}{1}\ \frac{2}{1}\ \frac{4}{1}\ \frac{4}{1}\ \frac{3}{1}\ \frac{5}{1}\ \frac{4}{1}\ \frac{5}{1}\ \frac{4}{1}\ \frac{2}{1}\ \frac{4}{1}\ \frac{3}{1}\ \frac{4}{1}\ \frac{4}{1}\ \frac{1}{1}\ \frac{4}{1}\ \frac{4}{1}\ \frac{3}{1}\ \frac{4}{1}\ \frac{4}{1}\ \frac{2}{1}\ \frac{4}{1}\ \frac{4}{1}\ \frac{3}{1}$$

$$\frac{5}{1}\ \frac{5}{1}\ \frac{2}{1}\ \frac{5}{1}\ \frac{5}{1}\ \frac{5}{1}\ \frac{3}{1}\ \frac{5}{1}\ \frac{2}{1}\ \frac{4}{1}\ \frac{5}{1}\ \frac{2}{1}\ \frac{5}{1}\ \frac{4}{1}\ \frac{5}{1}\ \frac{1}{1}\ \frac{5}{1}\ \frac{3}{1}\ \frac{4}{1}\ \frac{5}{1}\ \frac{5}{1}\ \frac{3}{1}\ \frac{5}{1}\ \frac{2}{1}$$

$$\frac{6}{1}\ \frac{6}{1}\ \frac{4}{1}\ \frac{6}{1}\ \frac{6}{1}\ \frac{3}{1}\ \frac{5}{1}\ \frac{6}{1}\ \frac{6}{1}\ \frac{2}{1}\ \frac{6}{1}\ \frac{4}{1}\ \frac{1}{1}\ \frac{6}{1}\ \frac{6}{1}\ \frac{5}{1}\ \frac{6}{1}\ \frac{3}{1}\ \frac{4}{1}\ \frac{6}{1}\ \frac{3}{1}\ \frac{6}{1}\ \frac{4}{1}\ \frac{6}{1}$$

$$\frac{7}{1}\ \frac{7}{1}\ \frac{2}{1}\ \frac{7}{1}\ \frac{7}{1}\ \frac{3}{1}\ \frac{7}{1}\ \frac{6}{1}\ \frac{7}{1}\ \frac{4}{1}\ \frac{7}{1}\ \frac{5}{1}\ \frac{7}{1}\ \frac{3}{1}\ \frac{4}{1}\ \frac{7}{1}\ \frac{7}{1}\ \frac{5}{1}\ \frac{7}{1}\ \frac{6}{1}\ \frac{7}{1}\ \frac{6}{1}\ \frac{7}{1}\ \frac{7}{1}$$

$$\frac{8}{1}\ \frac{8}{1}\ \frac{1}{1}\ \frac{8}{1}\ \frac{2}{1}\ \frac{8}{1}\ \frac{8}{1}\ \frac{3}{1}\ \frac{8}{1}\ \frac{8}{1}\ \frac{4}{1}\ \frac{5}{1}\ \frac{8}{1}\ \frac{5}{1}\ \frac{6}{1}\ \frac{8}{1}\ \frac{6}{1}\ \frac{4}{1}\ \frac{8}{1}\ \frac{7}{1}\ \frac{8}{1}\ \frac{4}{1}\ \frac{8}{1}\ \frac{9}{1}$$

$$\frac{9}{1}\ \frac{9}{1}\ \frac{3}{1}\ \frac{9}{1}\ \frac{9}{1}\ \frac{4}{1}\ \frac{9}{1}\ \frac{5}{1}\ \frac{9}{1}\ \frac{3}{1}\ \frac{9}{1}\ \frac{6}{1}\ \frac{9}{1}\ \frac{5}{1}\ \frac{9}{1}\ \frac{7}{1}\ \frac{9}{1}\ \frac{6}{1}\ \frac{9}{1}\ \frac{8}{1}\ \frac{9}{1}\ \frac{4}{1}\ \frac{9}{1}\ \frac{8}{1}$$

$$\frac{1}{1}\ \frac{2}{1}\ \frac{2}{1}\ \frac{1}{1}\ \frac{1}{1}\ \frac{5}{1}\ \frac{3}{1}\ \frac{1}{1}\ \frac{6}{1}\ \frac{3}{1}\ \frac{1}{1}\ \frac{4}{1}\ \frac{5}{1}\ \frac{1}{1}\ \frac{3}{1}\ \frac{6}{1}\ \frac{2}{1}\ \frac{4}{1}\ \frac{1}{1}\ \frac{7}{1}\ \frac{5}{1}\ \frac{1}{1}\ \frac{4}{1}\ \frac{6}{1}$$

$$\frac{3}{1}\ \frac{4}{1}\ \frac{2}{1}\ \frac{5}{1}\ \frac{4}{1}\ \frac{3}{1}\ \frac{3}{1}\ \frac{5}{1}\ \frac{2}{1}\ \frac{6}{1}\ \frac{1}{1}\ \frac{7}{1}\ \frac{7}{1}\ \frac{1}{1}\ \frac{6}{1}\ \frac{7}{1}\ \frac{5}{1}\ \frac{3}{1}\ \frac{4}{1}\ \frac{5}{1}\ \frac{3}{1}\ \frac{6}{1}\ \frac{2}{1}\ \frac{7}{1}$$

$$\frac{1}{1}\ \frac{8}{1}\ \frac{8}{1}\ \frac{1}{1}\ \frac{7}{1}\ \frac{2}{1}\ \frac{6}{1}\ \frac{3}{1}\ \frac{5}{1}\ \frac{4}{1}\ \frac{4}{1}\ \frac{6}{1}\ \frac{3}{1}\ \frac{7}{1}\ \frac{2}{1}\ \frac{8}{1}\ \frac{1}{1}\ \frac{9}{1}\ \frac{8}{1}\ \frac{2}{1}\ \frac{7}{1}\ \frac{3}{1}\ \frac{6}{1}\ \frac{4}{1}$$

$$\frac{5}{1}\ \frac{6}{1}\ \frac{4}{1}\ \frac{7}{1}\ \frac{3}{1}\ \frac{8}{1}\ \frac{2}{1}\ \frac{9}{1}\ \frac{8}{1}\ \frac{3}{1}\ \frac{7}{1}\ \frac{4}{1}\ \frac{6}{1}\ \frac{5}{1}\ \frac{5}{1}\ \frac{7}{1}\ \frac{4}{1}\ \frac{8}{1}\ \frac{3}{1}\ \frac{9}{1}\ \frac{8}{1}\ \frac{4}{1}\ \frac{7}{1}\ \frac{5}{1}$$

$$\frac{6}{1}\ \frac{7}{1}\ \frac{5}{1}\ \frac{8}{1}\ \frac{4}{1}\ \frac{9}{1}\ \frac{8}{1}\ \frac{5}{1}\ \frac{7}{1}\ \frac{6}{1}\ \frac{6}{1}\ \frac{8}{1}\ \frac{5}{1}\ \frac{9}{1}\ \frac{8}{1}\ \frac{6}{1}\ \frac{7}{1}\ \frac{8}{1}\ \frac{6}{1}\ \frac{9}{1}\ \frac{8}{1}\ \frac{7}{1}\ \frac{7}{1}\ \frac{9}{1}$$

Random Combinations: (count in 2, 3, and 4 measure groupings)

$$\frac{2}{1}\ \frac{1}{1}\ \frac{2}{1}\ \frac{2}{1}\ \frac{3}{1}\ \frac{4}{1}\ \frac{2}{1}\ \frac{1}{1}\ \frac{2}{1}\ \frac{3}{1}\ \frac{2}{1}\ \frac{4}{1}\ \frac{1}{1}\ \frac{2}{1}\ \frac{3}{1}\ \frac{2}{1}\ \frac{1}{1}\ \frac{2}{1}\ \frac{3}{1}\ \frac{2}{1}\ \frac{1}{1}\ \frac{2}{1}\ \frac{4}{1}\ \frac{2}{1}$$

$$\frac{3}{1}\ \frac{2}{1}\ \frac{3}{1}\ \frac{3}{1}\ \frac{3}{1}\ \frac{4}{1}\ \frac{3}{1}\ \frac{2}{1}\ \frac{3}{1}\ \frac{1}{1}\ \frac{3}{1}\ \frac{3}{1}\ \frac{4}{1}\ \frac{3}{1}\ \frac{1}{1}\ \frac{3}{1}\ \frac{3}{1}\ \frac{2}{1}\ \frac{3}{1}\ \frac{3}{1}\ \frac{4}{1}\ \frac{3}{1}\ \frac{2}{1}\ \frac{3}{1}$$

$$\frac{4}{1}\ \frac{2}{1}\ \frac{4}{1}\ \frac{4}{1}\ \frac{3}{1}\ \frac{5}{1}\ \frac{4}{1}\ \frac{5}{1}\ \frac{4}{1}\ \frac{2}{1}\ \frac{4}{1}\ \frac{3}{1}\ \frac{4}{1}\ \frac{4}{1}\ \frac{1}{1}\ \frac{4}{1}\ \frac{4}{1}\ \frac{3}{1}\ \frac{4}{1}\ \frac{4}{1}\ \frac{2}{1}\ \frac{4}{1}\ \frac{4}{1}\ \frac{3}{1}$$

$$\frac{5}{1}\ \frac{5}{1}\ \frac{2}{1}\ \frac{5}{1}\ \frac{5}{1}\ \frac{5}{1}\ \frac{3}{1}\ \frac{5}{1}\ \frac{2}{1}\ \frac{4}{1}\ \frac{5}{1}\ \frac{2}{1}\ \frac{5}{1}\ \frac{4}{1}\ \frac{5}{1}\ \frac{1}{1}\ \frac{5}{1}\ \frac{3}{1}\ \frac{4}{1}\ \frac{5}{1}\ \frac{5}{1}\ \frac{3}{1}\ \frac{5}{1}\ \frac{2}{1}$$

$$\frac{6}{1}\ \frac{6}{1}\ \frac{4}{1}\ \frac{6}{1}\ \frac{6}{1}\ \frac{3}{1}\ \frac{5}{1}\ \frac{6}{1}\ \frac{6}{1}\ \frac{2}{1}\ \frac{6}{1}\ \frac{4}{1}\ \frac{1}{1}\ \frac{6}{1}\ \frac{6}{1}\ \frac{5}{1}\ \frac{6}{1}\ \frac{3}{1}\ \frac{4}{1}\ \frac{6}{1}\ \frac{3}{1}\ \frac{6}{1}\ \frac{4}{1}\ \frac{6}{1}$$

$$\frac{7}{1}\ \frac{7}{1}\ \frac{2}{1}\ \frac{7}{1}\ \frac{7}{1}\ \frac{3}{1}\ \frac{7}{1}\ \frac{6}{1}\ \frac{7}{1}\ \frac{4}{1}\ \frac{7}{1}\ \frac{5}{1}\ \frac{7}{1}\ \frac{3}{1}\ \frac{4}{1}\ \frac{7}{1}\ \frac{7}{1}\ \frac{5}{1}\ \frac{7}{1}\ \frac{6}{1}\ \frac{7}{1}\ \frac{6}{1}\ \frac{7}{1}\ \frac{7}{1}$$

$$\frac{8}{1}\ \frac{8}{1}\ \frac{1}{1}\ \frac{8}{1}\ \frac{2}{1}\ \frac{8}{1}\ \frac{8}{1}\ \frac{3}{1}\ \frac{8}{1}\ \frac{8}{1}\ \frac{4}{1}\ \frac{5}{1}\ \frac{8}{1}\ \frac{5}{1}\ \frac{6}{1}\ \frac{8}{1}\ \frac{6}{1}\ \frac{4}{1}\ \frac{8}{1}\ \frac{7}{1}\ \frac{8}{1}\ \frac{4}{1}\ \frac{8}{1}\ \frac{9}{1}$$

$$\frac{9}{1}\ \frac{9}{1}\ \frac{3}{1}\ \frac{9}{1}\ \frac{9}{1}\ \frac{4}{1}\ \frac{9}{1}\ \frac{5}{1}\ \frac{9}{1}\ \frac{3}{1}\ \frac{9}{1}\ \frac{6}{1}\ \frac{9}{1}\ \frac{5}{1}\ \frac{9}{1}\ \frac{7}{1}\ \frac{9}{1}\ \frac{6}{1}\ \frac{9}{1}\ \frac{8}{1}\ \frac{9}{1}\ \frac{4}{1}\ \frac{9}{1}\ \frac{8}{1}$$

$$\frac{1}{1}\ \frac{2}{1}\ \frac{2}{1}\ \frac{1}{1}\ \frac{5}{1}\ \frac{3}{1}\ \frac{1}{1}\ \frac{6}{1}\ \frac{3}{1}\ \frac{1}{1}\ \frac{4}{1}\ \frac{5}{1}\ \frac{1}{1}\ \frac{3}{1}\ \frac{6}{1}\ \frac{2}{1}\ \frac{4}{1}\ \frac{1}{1}\ \frac{7}{1}\ \frac{5}{1}\ \frac{1}{1}\ \frac{4}{1}\ \frac{6}{1}$$

$$\frac{3}{1}\ \frac{4}{1}\ \frac{2}{1}\ \frac{5}{1}\ \frac{4}{1}\ \frac{3}{1}\ \frac{3}{1}\ \frac{5}{1}\ \frac{2}{1}\ \frac{6}{1}\ \frac{1}{1}\ \frac{7}{1}\ \frac{7}{1}\ \frac{1}{1}\ \frac{6}{1}\ \frac{7}{1}\ \frac{5}{1}\ \frac{3}{1}\ \frac{4}{1}\ \frac{5}{1}\ \frac{3}{1}\ \frac{6}{1}\ \frac{2}{1}\ \frac{7}{1}$$

$$\frac{1}{1}\ \frac{8}{1}\ \frac{8}{1}\ \frac{1}{1}\ \frac{7}{1}\ \frac{2}{1}\ \frac{6}{1}\ \frac{3}{1}\ \frac{5}{1}\ \frac{4}{1}\ \frac{4}{1}\ \frac{6}{1}\ \frac{3}{1}\ \frac{7}{1}\ \frac{2}{1}\ \frac{8}{1}\ \frac{1}{1}\ \frac{9}{1}\ \frac{8}{1}\ \frac{2}{1}\ \frac{7}{1}\ \frac{3}{1}\ \frac{6}{1}\ \frac{4}{1}$$

$$\frac{5}{1}\ \frac{6}{1}\ \frac{4}{1}\ \frac{7}{1}\ \frac{3}{1}\ \frac{8}{1}\ \frac{2}{1}\ \frac{9}{1}\ \frac{8}{1}\ \frac{3}{1}\ \frac{7}{1}\ \frac{4}{1}\ \frac{6}{1}\ \frac{5}{1}\ \frac{5}{1}\ \frac{7}{1}\ \frac{4}{1}\ \frac{8}{1}\ \frac{3}{1}\ \frac{9}{1}\ \frac{8}{1}\ \frac{4}{1}\ \frac{7}{1}\ \frac{5}{1}$$

$$\frac{6}{1}\ \frac{7}{1}\ \frac{5}{1}\ \frac{8}{1}\ \frac{4}{1}\ \frac{9}{1}\ \frac{8}{1}\ \frac{5}{1}\ \frac{7}{1}\ \frac{6}{1}\ \frac{6}{1}\ \frac{8}{1}\ \frac{5}{1}\ \frac{9}{1}\ \frac{8}{1}\ \frac{6}{1}\ \frac{7}{1}\ \frac{8}{1}\ \frac{6}{1}\ \frac{9}{1}\ \frac{8}{1}\ \frac{7}{1}\ \frac{7}{1}\ \frac{9}{1}$$

From Section 1-1 to Section X-6

1. Perform all of the exercises as follows:

   A. Clap the rhythmic patterns and count aloud using any acceptable counting system (metronome clicking the pulse).

   B. Conduct the meter signatures, count aloud, and tap the rhythmic patterns (metronome clicking the pulse).

   C. Conduct the meter signatures and verbalize the rhythmic patterns using any articulate sounds, i.e., ta, da, etc. (metronome clicking the pulse).

   D. Perform A. through C. without the metronome.

2. Change pace, add accents and dynamics.

Section I-No division of pulse and division of pulse into two equal durations

Section I-1

Section I-2

Section I-3

Section I-4

Section I-5

Section I-6

Section I-7

Section I-8 Ametric

Section I-9

Section I-10

Section I-11

Section I-12

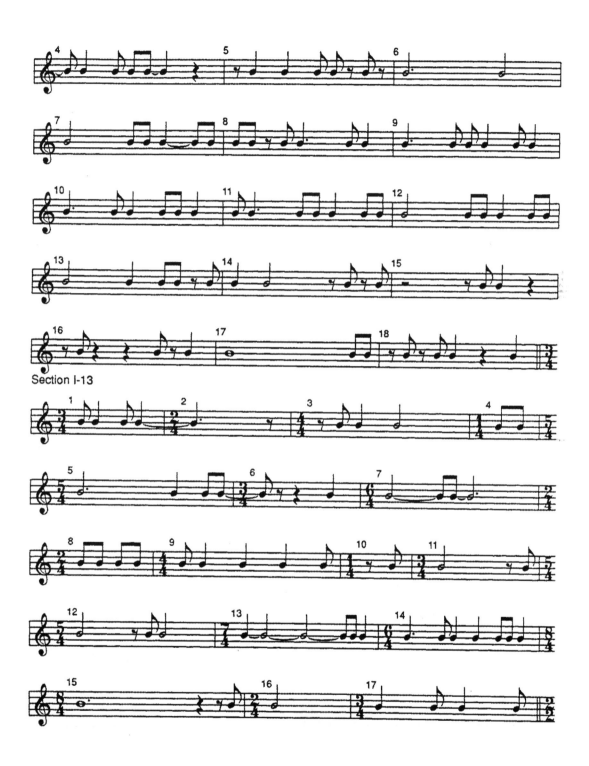

Section I-13

Section I-14

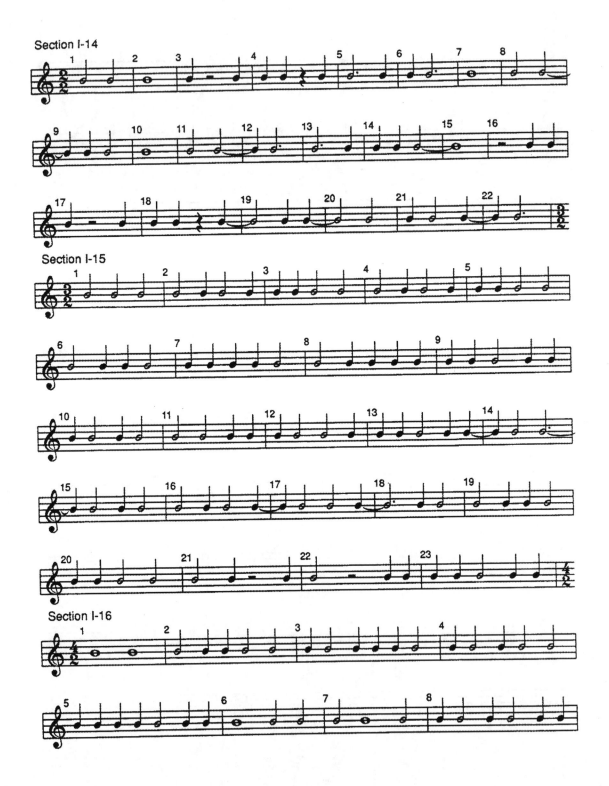

Section I-15

Section I-16

- 44 -

Section I-17

Section II

ENERGY IS...

Energy is expressed in all matter and life. We lie in an ocean of motion. Motion is the manifestation of energy. Change is its attribute. Energy of position, such as a storm forming in the distance, represents potential energy. Dedicated practice and superior performance are a result of taking latent potential energies and turning them into available, active, positive, kinetic energies. The passage of potential energies to actual energies is **an intense, sweat-producing, exhausting experience! J.B.**

Energy is that which causes movement in material bodies. That movement may be of varying proportions in time and distance. It is often thought that energy is flowing in only one direction that is, dissipating. But in fact it is both dissipating and accumulating and these forces are in balance with each other. Because these forces are always in balance, there will also be a balanced reaction to all causes.

In creating sound, the energy expressed is equal to that which is conceived to be expressed. Thus, to change the desire level of those who are listening to a performance, change the energy level of those who are creating the performance. H.R.D.

Student Definitions:

...Energy is the potential force inherent within. Energy itself cannot be seen, though we can see, hear, feel and imagine its power. Inner energy is vital... when my energy level is high, I am productive. I feel motivated and positive. Increased awareness of energy and its effect on life can facilitate the realization of the potential within...

...Energy is the ability to do work. The amount of energy in the universe is always the same. You can only get as much out of something as you put into it. Looking at this definition in terms of musical performance, it stands to reason that you will only get as much out of a performance as you put into it... The energy of movement is the energy needed to produce a satisfactory musical performance. The energy that turns notes and rhythms into music is not physical, but mental and emotional...The potential for the expression of these mental and emotional energies is in everyone; it just needs a spark to jump the gap. The search for this spark is a never ending journey through your own personal maze of doubts, insecurities, and inhibitions. Some of us achieve it momentarily; a lucky few sustain it for a lifetime...

...In order to cause a sound wave to travel in a medium, work has to be done to produce it. Power is the rate at which work is done or the rate at which energy is being used up or radiated. The energy of a sound wave is directly proportional to the square of the amplitude times the frequency. The greater the amplitude and frequency, the greater the amount of energy being spent, and the more intense the sound. Energy then determines the quality of the sound being made, and in the case of the musician, that quality is significant to say the least. Even soft sounds must be convincing and that requires as much energy as a sforzando. Energy is that potential force that drives music forward in time...

...When I think of energy, I think of excitement. When there is low or no apparent energy, there is no excitement. I am thinking of a choir that I direct. When there is energy or excitement or enthusiasm in the sound, it is full of life. The sounds are on pitch. It is interesting to listen to. When the choir is tired or distracted or not concentrating, the sound is dull and flat. The notes are under pitch. The sound is not interesting to listen to. I often tell them, particularly when we are singing a soft passage, to keep the energy in the sound. Energy is present in performance.

Sometimes we say "the adrenaline is flowing". If the energy is not controlled, it becomes stage fright, and taken to the extreme, can destroy a performance. If it can be controlled, it can lend sparkle and vivacity to the performance...

...Energy is the ability to do work. It is constant; it cannot be created or destroyed. But it can change from one form to another. Therein lies an essential key to quality musical performance...Despite energetic surroundings, it seems that most of us function by tapping just enough energy to get by. Only a few people seem to have harnessed their own energy and made use of the surrounding energy to reach their goals. Many of us seem to leave the bulk of our energy to channel itself into mindless functions or mere habits, be they good or bad. Only through a determined course of increased awareness and concentration can we begin to use our energy to improve our musical performances. There must be decided effort to maintain high energy in musical practice. Rather than wasting energy flogging ourselves and acting embarrassed over "silly" mistakes, we could use that same energy to conduct a cool, objective survey of the problems in our playing. Rather than squandering energy by voraciously attacking a new or difficult passage, we could gain enough control over our energy to calmly assess what is required to play the passage well...

Section II-Division of pulse into three and four equal durations

Section II-1

Section II-2

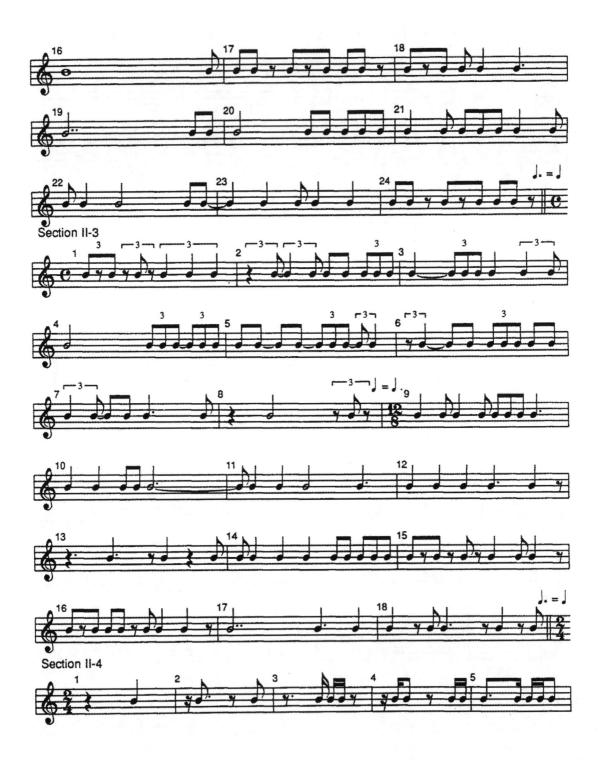

Section II-3

Section II-4

Section II-5

Section II-6

Section II-7

Section II-8 Ametric

Section II-9 Coordination Duet

Section II-10 Coordination Duet

Section II-11 Quartet

Section III

CONCENTRATION IS...

Concentration is the act of drawing or directing your thoughts to a common center, thereby focusing the powers of your mind and making possible much more intense action. Concentration depends, in part, upon how much you desire your object of attainment. Dedicated practice and superior performance are a result of the ability to maintain a high level of concentration. J.B.

Concentration comes from the desire of mind to express materiality. Its antonym is the word "decentration" which expresses the desire to express non-materiality and timelessness. For instance, in order to compose music, one must lose awareness of the senses. Then one will become aware of concepts and ideas. From these, one begins to concentrate to form bodies for these thoughts by using learned techniques and through physical effort to put these into music notation which can then be performed. H.R.D.

Student Definitions:

...The Latin origin of the term concentration refers to that which has a common center, and is best expressed by the term, "one pointedness." Imagine that you have an unsharpened pencil or a small stick. If you had to use either of them to pierce a piece of cardboard, you will find it difficult until the ends of your simple implements have been properly sharpened. Even if considerable pressure is exerted on an unsharpened pencil it will not produce a neat hole. Why? Because a simple physical law is at work. The power has been dissipated over the whole surface of the instrument, thus providing insufficient force to separate and remove the particles of cardboard and form a clean hole. An average man's mind is filled with countless thoughts, and therefore each individual thought is extremely weak. When in place of these many useless thoughts, there appears only one, it is a power in itself and has a wide influence...

...There are several lessons to be learned about our ability to concentrate from the art of transcendental meditation. First there is the inherent idea that thought can be powerful. Second, thought requires physical energy. Third, powerful thoughts come to be such through the channeling of the physical energy and the entire consciousness into that one thought. Extraneous thoughts will weaken the powerful thought, thus the ability to concentrate. The role of concentration in all aspects of musicianship is vital. It leads to the most profound form of communication conceivable. In a performance, a musician is mentally and physically absorbed in the music. He/she isn't even aware that an audience is there. The music transcends that gap between the musician and the listener. Without saying a word, or even being aware of another's presence, the performer reveals their being to a complete stranger...

...Too often we try to pay attention to too many things at once. The result is that we begin to feel confused and out of control; things happen too fast. We end up jumping from one thing to another without any feeling of real accomplishment. The practical application of concentration is to overcome the distractions caused by your environment, your own lack of confidence and any other concerns...

...Without concentration the human potential lies dormant beneath the level of conscious, creative, fulfilled and effective living. Concentration is depth of thought. It is the disciplined centering of one's attention upon a task deemed significant enough to draw a person into himself, and then releasing him outward. Concentration is the process of the orderly application of the human mind to the performance of a task; solving a problem; achieving a specific goal through systematic study, making something or someone the center of attention; disciplined specialization...

...Concentration involves a balanced awareness of self and surroundings, with an easy emphasis on whatever is particularly relevant at the moment...

...Concentration is the act of directing one's energy towards a common center or objective. Children in a classroom are described as being "on task"; adults describe the act of concentration as focusing or centering in. Self-discipline is another key word in defining concentration. One must have the desire to put their mind to a certain task (self or external motivation)...

...Concentration requires both a focus (short or long termed) and motivation...

...Our ability to concentrate enables us to learn. Without the ability to concentrate all other musical abilities are useless. Concentration is our greatest tool for combating nervousness--distracting thoughts cannot interfere with our music making...

...Concentration is exclusive attention to one object; it is the closed mental application applied with all of one's attention. It is the mental act of drawing or focusing all energies toward a common point of union. It is complete mental control which forces all surrounding, disturbing elements so far into the background that when one is fully engrossed in the process, he is alone in the pursuit of his goal...

...Concentration is a fascination of the mind. It is the ability to be totally involved in one thing at a time. ATTRACTION-a key word. Our attention cannot be kept still if what we focus upon is not attractive to us and we perceive it as less than interesting. Lack of interest leads to lack of CONCIOUSNESS. To solve this problem we need to involve ourselves if merely listening or "playing through" was not doing the trick. Ask questions, take notes, OBSERVE. BE the music. Eventually, we become so involved, "in the groove," and on top of things that our minds are totally fascinated with what is happening here and now, rather than worrying about the past, present or future...

...Concentration is the focusing of energies on a common center. To concentrate effectively, the mind must be cleared of extraneous thoughts and distractions. Once the mind is ready to work, it is to our benefit to have a "plan of attack." 1) What am I doing? 2) What do I want to do? 3) Am I now doing what I want to do? In order to come up with an agenda for detailed practice, play through the piece or passage once, careful to note (even mark) areas that need work. The agenda can include missed notes, rhythms, or dynamics; lack/overuse of expressiveness; or lack of appropriate phrasing to name a few. The physical and mental energies can now be centered on a set of specific problems...

...Concentration is the focusing of the mind on a particular object of thought, thus reducing to a minimum the effects of other stimuli. The distractions which must be overcome may originate internally (butterflies, headache, and stray thoughts) or externally, (coughing audience, equipment problems, and environmental quirks)...

...Concentration may allow a teacher to listen to an eight bar phrase played by 90 seventh graders. The teacher needs the ability to hear the F sharp missed by the trumpets in bar one, the B flat missed by the flutes in bar 2, the missed cymbal crash in bar 3, the dotted eighth and 16th note pattern missed in bar 5 and the fact that the flutes finally played the G flat in tune in measure 8. This information may be relayed to the class when they return from the fire drill...

Section III-Division of pulse into three through nine equal durations

Section III-1

Section III-2

Section III-3

Section III-4

Section III-5

Section III-6

Section III-7

Section III-8 Ametric

Section III-9 Ametric

Section III-10 Ametric

Section III-11 Quartet

Section IV

CONFIDENCE IS...

Confidence is a firm trust, reliance, an assurance, and a certainty of belief in your own abilities and talents. When you are reaching toward a certain goal, your success is in part a result of maintaining your self-confidence regardless of all inevitable problems, circumstances, and obstacles. Through self-confidence as a performer or teacher, you will find one of the secrets for reaching success. J.B.

Confidence in the performance of music comes from a combination of basic talent, the quantity and quality of instruction received, and the quantity and quality of practice devoted to learning one's instrument and music. H.R.D.

Student Definitions:

...Confidence is the quality of being certain. Every time you perform and make mistakes, you realize that the world does not end because of your errors. When you are not overly concerned with mistakes, you start to relax, and the number of mistakes actually decreases. It is the fear of the mistake that in itself creates the mistake.

The primary purpose of music is to communicate; a wrong note in itself will not interfere with that communication. What will interfere with it is your lack of control over your emotions when that mistake occurs. If your confidence in yourself is sufficiently developed, you will retain your concentration level and your message will still come across, and just as important, your self-esteem will remain intact...

...Confidence is: 1. a state of mind 2. faith in one's ability to perform a task 3. never saying maybe (think of the anti-perspirant commercial that says raise your hand if you're SURE) 4. the desire to accomplish a goal. Confidence in performance arises from: 1. thorough knowledge of the music 2. faith in that knowledge as certain and unchanging...

...Confidence is a vital process of mental and spiritual alteration whereby the individual shifts from a concept of self-limitation to that of self-improvement, from deterioration to growth, from failure to accomplishment...

...Confidence does more to make conversation than wit. When the various meanings of confidence are distinguished and clarified, the main elements remain: seeking of firm truth through presence, profoundness, trust, self-assuredness, and belief. Other definitions of confidence include: sharing or trusted with private opinions; implies a strong but not haughty belief...

...Confidence as it relates to the performance of music means the self-assurance or self-belief in one's ability to perform in an acceptable manner the music one is performing. Self-esteem and ability are the dependent factors which make up a confident performance...

...My experiences have led me to believe that music is a very negatively taught art. Criticism is administered like bad medicine to make you well, but it seems to instill a feeling of inadequacy which directly diminishes self-esteem. We need to review our manner of learning so that it is not a series of tests where we succeed or fail but rather a gradual process of growing. In this, a kind of growth lays a secure confidence in ourselves and a striving to be better musicians. When we free ourselves of this fear of failure we can begin to feel confident with our own progression of learning and approach our music with confidence and a willingness to make a few mistakes along the way to a better understanding of our art...

...Confidence is a mental state wherein one feels sure of one's abilities. The prerequisite for confidence is the ability to concentrate. Janos Starker, a concert cellist, once stated that confidence is acquired when, in practice, something is done correctly at least 99% of the time. It is true that all technical problems should be ironed out, but it is also true that he/she must be able to drive out all thoughts of possible defeats during performance...

...Confidence is the state of mind a person achieves when doubts and inhibitions have been put aside. I contend that to communicate with others, you must have communication within yourself. The self assurance of knowing your own capabilities and levels of achievement lead to a confidence in performance which cannot be daunted by human error or unexpected disturbances. Confidence includes the inner knowledge that circumstances cannot be totally controlled, and that one's best effort is able to stand by its own merit. A truly confident person is relaxed even in the face of difficult sight-reading because he or she has the tools to work with new and unexpected material...

..Confidence is a portion of one's self-esteem. Self-esteem includes essentials for life such as love, respect, recognition for real worth and talents, and a pride in belonging. **People with confidence are winners.** Confident people are self-directed. They choose their path. They are self-reliant and take the responsibility to get a job done successfully. They keep themselves moving in their chosen direction by a clear set of goals. They learn from their mistakes, and use this as a form of growth. When one has confidence, he can channel his abilities to perform and teach with utmost potential. Confident people have the ability to communicate their knowledge and skills to others...

Section IV-Using eighth note pulses

Section IV-3

Section IV-4

Section IV-5 Ametric

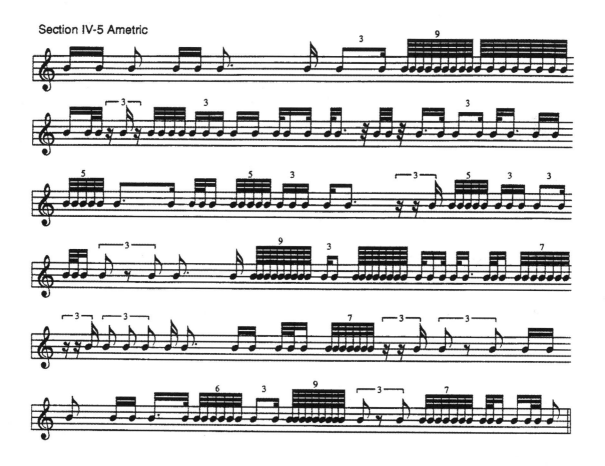

Section IV-6 Coordination Duet

Section IV-7 Quartet

Section V

COORDINATION IS...

In music, coordination is the act of combining mental and physical procedures into one harmonious interaction. Coordination involves learning on the conscious level through careful repetition that can then be performed automatically. For a musician, good coordination becomes a product of many hours spent in careful practice. J.B.

Coordination is driving a stick shift car. The separate limbs of the body work independently of one another in order to bring about a desired result. Coordination involves translating mental knowledge into physical action and that becomes difficult when the physical action requires several body parts to function independently of one another. It is not enough for the performer to know how to perform a specific technique on his instrument; he has to translate that knowledge into physical action. This comes from practice until the feel of the motion becomes natural or automatic. H.R.D.

Student Definitions:

...Coordination is an intentional, purposeful action. It does not happen by accident. It is not haphazard...

...In music, coordination involves physical and mental states acting together. The mental activity must coordinate concentration, the mathematical level of rhythm, energy level, and steady time...

...Coordination is the act of bringing together independent muscular motions for the accomplishment of a single task. This involvement could hardly take place without the involvement of the mind as well. Within the mind there must be coordination to enable the impulses and thoughts and choices happen simultaneously...

...Coordination calls upon our mind skills of concentration, our use and understanding of energy as it would apply here, and a whole bunch of practice...

...To be coordinated is to be able to have more than one thing going on at the same time with equal independence. In thinking about music, one must be able to translate what the brain perceives into action. Coordination is orderly and precise not haphazard. In terms of rhythm, it begins with an understanding of the basic mathematical relationships of the notated page. From that perception, one must convert the mental image into physical action–whether it is speaking a rhythm, clapping a rhythm or playing the rhythm on an instrument. As the rhythms become more difficult, more time is needed to be able to instantaneously convert the mental image into the physical realm. Practice must begin slowly and gradually increase the speed to the desired tempo. One must program one's mind to perform a rhythm upon sight...

...Coordination for most inhabitants of this era involves much more than the alignment of physical functions. Coordination extends into scheduling, working among peers, and simply existing from day to day...

...To improve coordination, we must have a plan. Well-coordinated acts do not occur as a matter of chance. They are meticulously premeditated...

...The conductor or leader of any musical group is the person who is entrusted with the role of coordinating the whole. A leader must take the ideas and physical coordination of many different people and make them into an integrated unit. Viewed in this way it is amazing that anything ever gets done musically. I have just found new respect for conductors...

...Coordination is really what playing your instrument is all about. If you are a woodwind player, you must coordinate tonguing, finger combinations, and rhythmic accuracy. If you are a string player, you must coordinate the bowings with correct fingerings, rhythmic accuracy and balance. Actually, every musician has to coordinate physical and psychological factors so that he may play efficiently. The way to achieve coordination, for a musician, is to be very aware of all of the things that go on during practice. This involves rhythmic accuracy, tone quality, projection of line, correct notes, hand and body movements and thought patterns...

Section V-Using Sixteenth note pulses

Section V-3

Section V-4

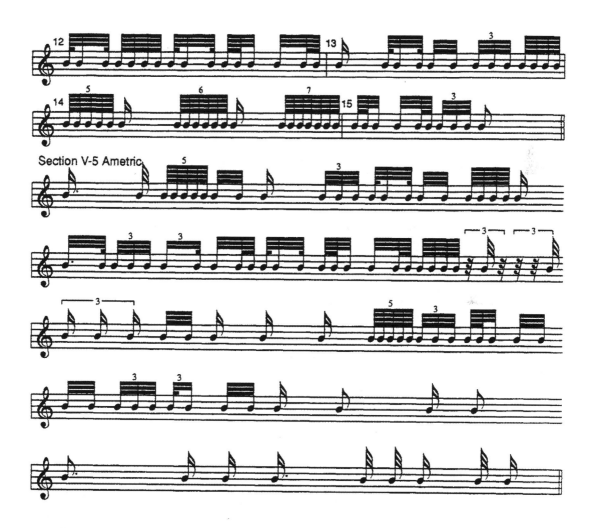

Section V-6 Coordination Duet

Section VI

CREATIVITY IS...

Creativity is the act of making something **"extra-ordinary"** out of the ordinary. That is precisely what you are doing now by studying this book. J.B.

Creativity is the ability to bring into the world ideas, concepts and thoughts which lead to a more balanced, efficient, and happier existence. Creativity can be demonstrated by anyone who helps to produce something of value even when the product is not originally their own concept. In the performance of music, we can express creativity by not only playing the notes correctly, but by delving beneath the surface of the music to try to express the thoughts that inspired the composer. H.R.D.

Student Definitions:

...Creativity includes the task of taking materials of one form and transforming those materials into something new and different from what they were before. Inherent in the act of creating is the element of purpose (on the part of the creator), the direct consequece of meaning, order and logic. In music, creativity operates on two levels. One of these is the level at which the musician transforms the written page of notation into audible sound. This level of creation is almost always considered re-creation. Here most of the imagination will be used only in an attempt to realize the original idea held by the composer. Taking liberties with the music that do not remain consistent with the composer's original idea is certainly being creative but, in my opinion, is inappropriate...

...Creativity is to bring into being through the inner application of individual ability something constructive, purposeful, worthwhile...

...Creativity is the unique ability to add to the ordinary an inventive, imaginative flair and thus make something new and unusual. It is easier to recognize creativity than it is to cultivate it, if it is possible to cultivate at all...

...Creativity is the means whereby a performer establishes an interpretive style and expresses his own individuality through the music...

...Creativity is a personal, inspired urge to produce something new. Music, art, and literature are often categorized as the creative arts because through them we are able to express ourselves as individuals. Our goal as musicians should be the attainment of a child-like newness in our approach to every performance—a goal that in and of itself is regenerative and life-giving...

...Probably the most creative people are those who work with children because children are so willing to accept the unusual. To the musician, creativity is making music with the unobvious or doing something different with the obvious (P.D.Q. Bach)...

...When we talk about "being creative," we usually mean taking something that is already present and changing it. This is what we mean when we talk about art, painting, sculpture or any other medium. When we think of composing music, it may be in any one of a myriad of styles. With music, we are taking what is already present—notes, rhythm, dynamics, etc., and re-arranging them to "create" or "compose" a piece of music. We sometimes talk about creating music when we play. Again, we are taking what is already there and using it to produce sound, even in improvisation. We are drawing on what we know—chords, rhythmic patterns, melodic patterns and then making new combinations...

...Some people are said to be creative. If you analyze what makes them unique or creative, it is that they are able to come up with ideas that fill a need or are different from the run-of-the-mill ideas. The creative teacher is one who looks for different ways of explaining the same things...

...Most of the time in school is spent memorizing facts and figures and answering questions based on these facts and figures. This is called cognitive and convergent thinking. However, it is also very important to learn to think divergently—to create new ideas and let your imagination soar! Imagination is the capacity to form mental pictures of past experiences, or to create mental pictures of situations or conditions that we have not actually experienced. Literature, music, painting, sculpture, and other arts enrich the lives of most people. Those in the fine arts and humanities are concerned with creating beauty and with expressing, studying, and preserving ideas and cultural values. **Students should leave our schools with their creative abilities aglow.** Creativity implies that leap of imagination and understanding which enables individuals to grow in dignity and purpose in the world. Creativity also implies the ability on the part of the creator to carry others with him in the endless quest for insight...

...To create is to bring one's own feelings and thoughts from within onto the page, canvas, or whatever the medium. An idea is a creation within the mind. How one brings this idea into creative fruition is up to the individual. The most effective creativity is that which is distinguishable by the style that accompanies it...

...Creativity is a gift within one that should be nurtured and developed. My creativity gets sparked into motivation by other's creativity and how they are expressing it. Some call this inspiration, and it can come from within as well, since our thoughts can inspire us...

...Creativity, in my view, should be encouraged in and outside of the class. The fact that others are bound to define it differently proves its very existence. Applying it to one's idiom is the fun and frustrating part, but certainly precious and valuable and the very thing that makes us love another's work all the more...

...Creativity is a term that can be associated with words like newness, unique, inspirational, imaginative, weird, different, extraordinary, individual, personal, inventive, expressive, profound, resourceful, interpretive, innocent, unusual, artsy, playful, explorative, and spiritual, just to name a few. Creativity, as it relates to music can mean a variety of things in itself. To a composer of music, creativity means writing from one's soul, along with one's learned application of musical knowledge, a new song, a musical score to a movie, a symphony, etc...

...Creativity, even to those who are blessed with an extra abundance of it, cannot ever be force-fed. It has to come naturally, without force, almost effortlessly...

...When a musician happens to be a performer, creativity takes on quite a different role. A performer in the classical music world is usually someone who plays a wide repertoire of compositions that he did not himself write. The job of the performer, then, is to develop an interpretive style of that composer's music, bringing to the music his/her own individual flair and expression of emotion the individual piece has to say. Generally, the performer tries to bring out in an individual way the original idea held by the composer. When the performer attempts to reach beyond and expands upon what was notated on the page by the composer, he often is involved in improvisation, which involves his own original musical ideas as well as those of the composer...

...Creativity in music or in any other field, particularly the arts, should be something that is fun and tied in with playfulness, as it so often is with kids. Adults who are able to continue their sense of playfulness from when they were kids into their adult lives are often the most highly creative of all people...

Section VI-Review

Section VI-1 Review

Section VI-2

Section VI-3

Section VI-4

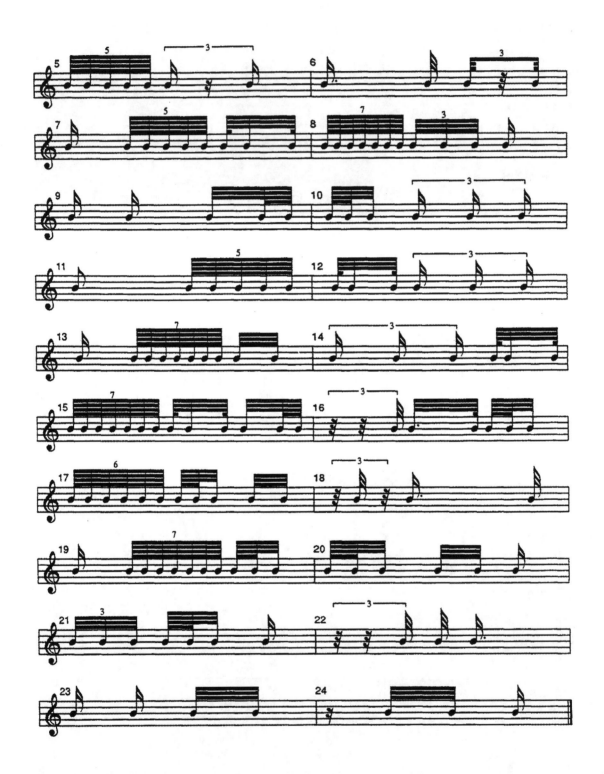

Section VII

In Jazz Style

The following rhythmic patterns should be performed in a jazz style and at a moderate pace. They should be interpreted in the following manner:

A. Pulse notes occurring on the pulse are played as noted:

B. The **point of articulation** for non-pulse notes occurring on the pulse is the **first note** of an **eighth note triplet**:

C. The **point of articulation** for **any note** occurring as an **upbeat** to a pulse is the **third note** of an eighth note triplet:

D. Notes occurring under triplet brackets are played as noted:

Section VII-1 Jazz Style

Section VII-3 Jazz Style

Section VII-4 Jazz Style

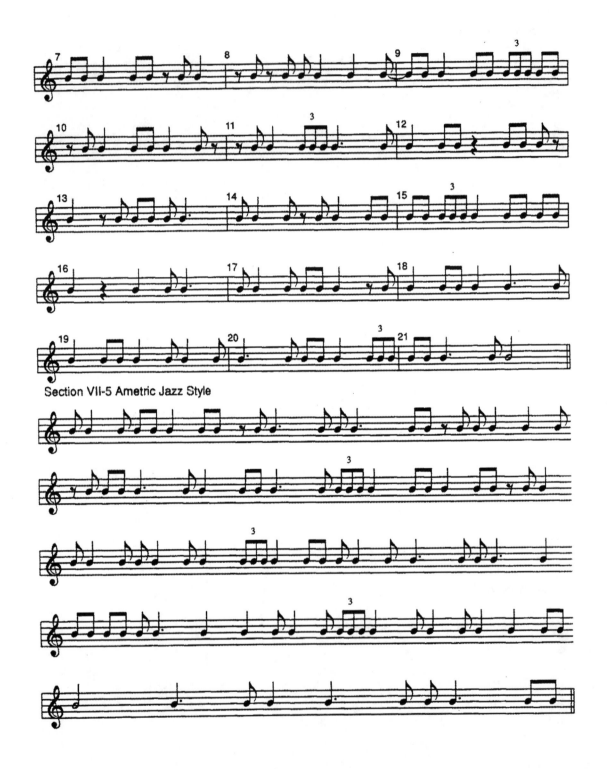

Section VII-5 Ametric Jazz Style

Section VII-6 Coordination Duet

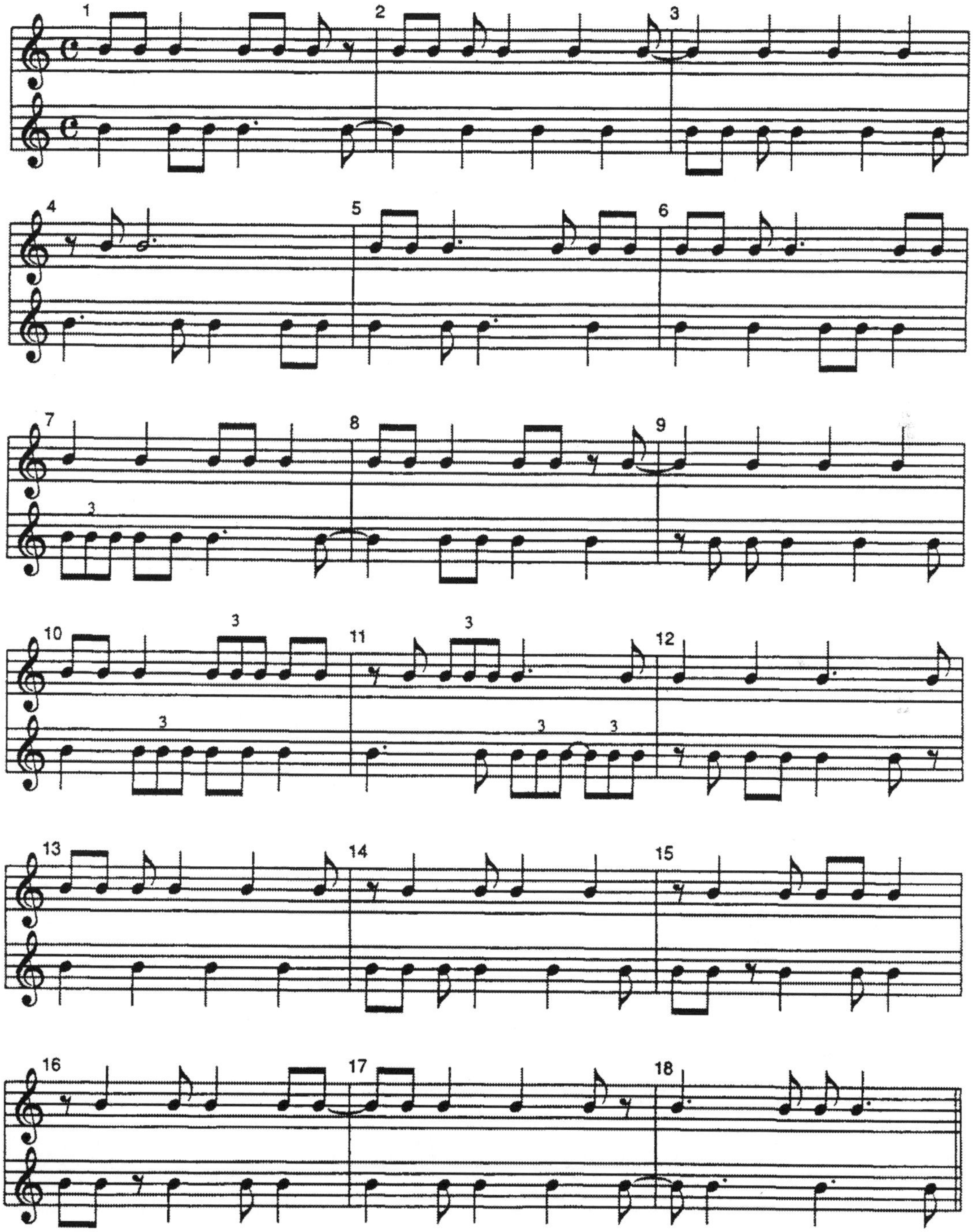

Section VII-7 Quartet

Section VIII

Changing rhythmic structures

Section VIII-3

Section VIII-4

Section VIII-5

Section VIII-6 Coordination Duet

Section IX

COUNTER RHYTHM
WORKSHEET

In counter rhythms (2:3, 3:4, etc.), the first number indicates how many equally spaced notes are to be performed. The second number indicates either how many pulse notes or how many equally spaced non-pulse notes are to be performed. In the following examples, a counter rhythm is produced when an equally spaced rhythmic pattern is combined with an equally spaced pulse.

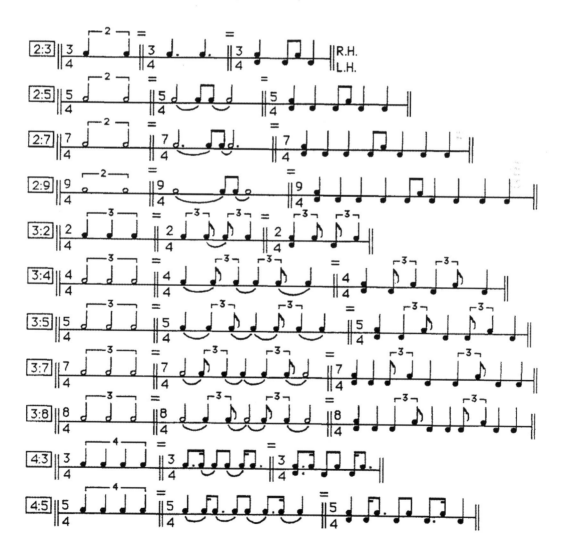

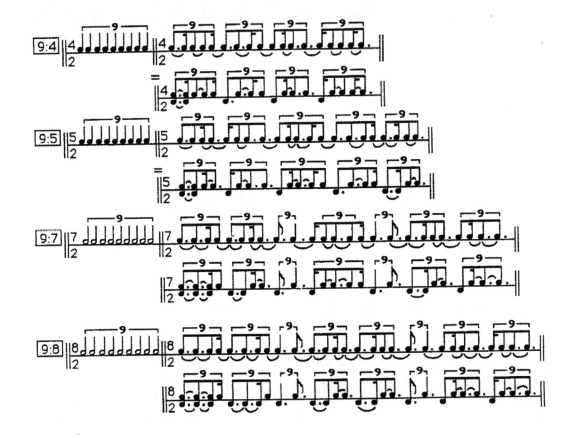

Section IX-Using counter rhythms

Section IX-3

Section IX-4

Section IX-5 Coordination Duet

Section IX-6 Quartet

Section X

Metric modulation and fractional meter signatures

Section X-2

Section X-3

How Good Is Your Rhythm?
Could You Use Some Help?

DVD LECTURE
Jack Bell

VIDEO EDITING
Howard Ryerson Davis III

Developing Rhythmic Sensitivity DVD Lecture

This two plus hour DVD is a comprehensive lecture and demonstration of the concepts necessary to accurately perform teach and notate rhythmic patterns.

The format and submenus of the DVD, professionally edited by the book's co-author, Howard Davis, follows the companion textbook and allows the student direct access to any topic of interest.

The DVD is a result of Mr. Bell successfully teaching the course Developing Rhythmic Sensitivity at Georgia State University for over 20 years.

TOPICS INCLUDE

CONCEPTS OF SOUND AND TIME
UNDERSTANDING METER, PACE AND ACCENTS
CONDUCTING IN RELATION TO METER SIGNATURES
PERFORMING JAZZ AND COUNTER RHYTHMS
HUNDREDS OF RHYTHMIC EXERCISES